for Pat, who loved color,
and for Sara & Sonia, who live in color,
so that no day is ever really gray

T. S. Poetry Press
New York
tspoetry.com

ISBN 978-1-943120-19-2

Library of Congress Control Number: 2017910202

Language Arts & Disciplines / Alphabets & Writing Systems
      A Is for Azure: The Alphabet in Colors
      Author, L.L. Barkat
      Illustrator, Donna Z. Falcone

Summary: Brilliant ink-on-tile illustrations bring the alphabet to colorful life. Children will delight in the rich, poetic language of colors like emerald, jasmine, and quartz—while also meeting old favorites like yellow, orange and purple.

Companion materials available at **tweetspeakpoetry.com/literacyextras**

A is for Azure

the alphabet in colors

by l. l. barkat

illustrated by donna z. falcone

ts ❤ *literacy starts with love*

A is for azure

an azure sky

B is for brass

a brass-petaled field

c is for cranberry

a cranberry twirl

D is for denim

a denim-blue sea

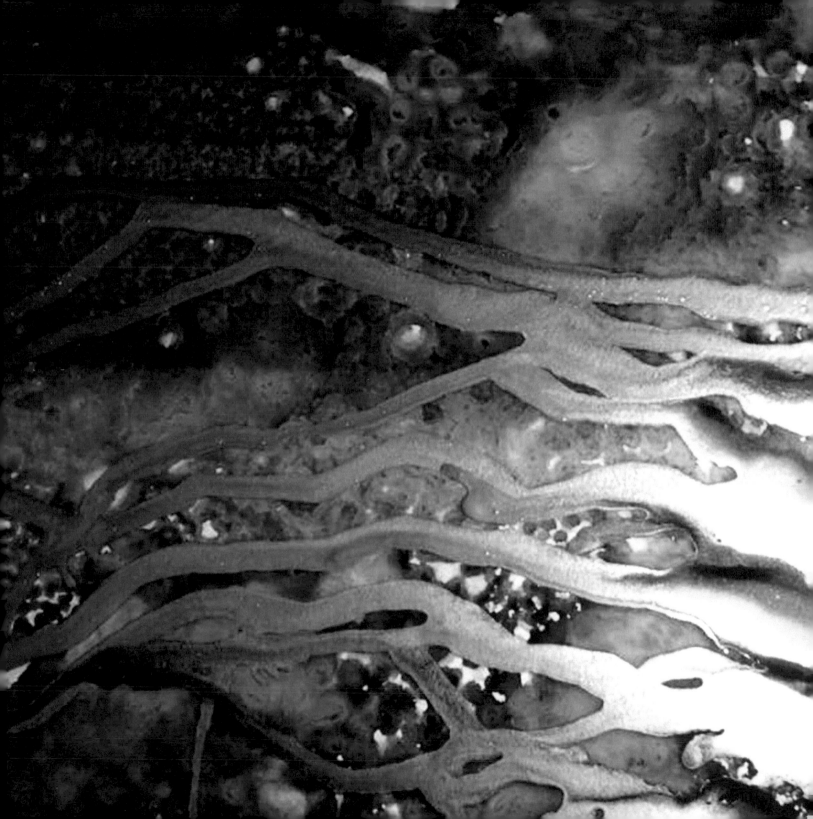

E is for emerald

an emerald fir

F is for fuchsia

a fuchsia heart

G is for green

a green rolling hill

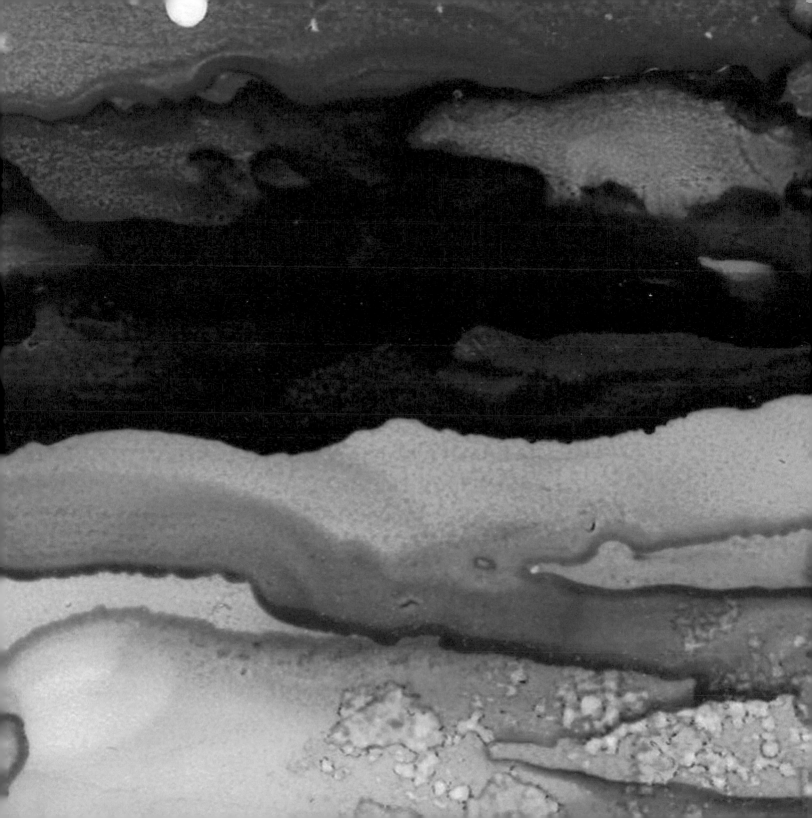

H is for heliotrope

a heliotrope trio

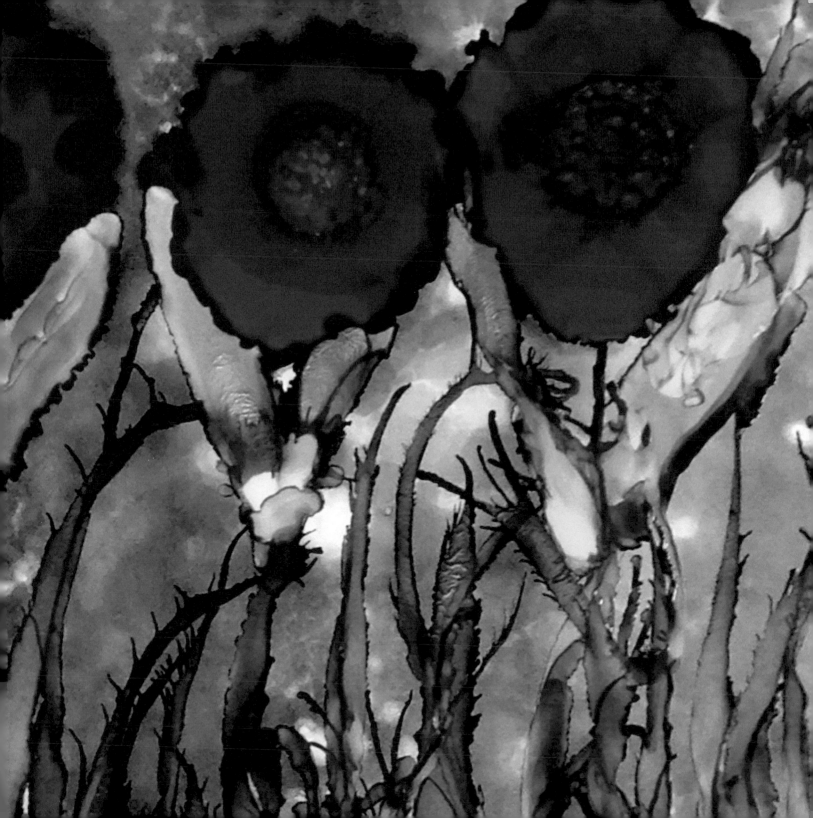

I is for iceberg

an iceberg stream

J is for jasmine

a jasmine coil

k is for kiwi

a kiwi fish

L is for lilac

a lilac frill

M is for midnight

a midnight terrain

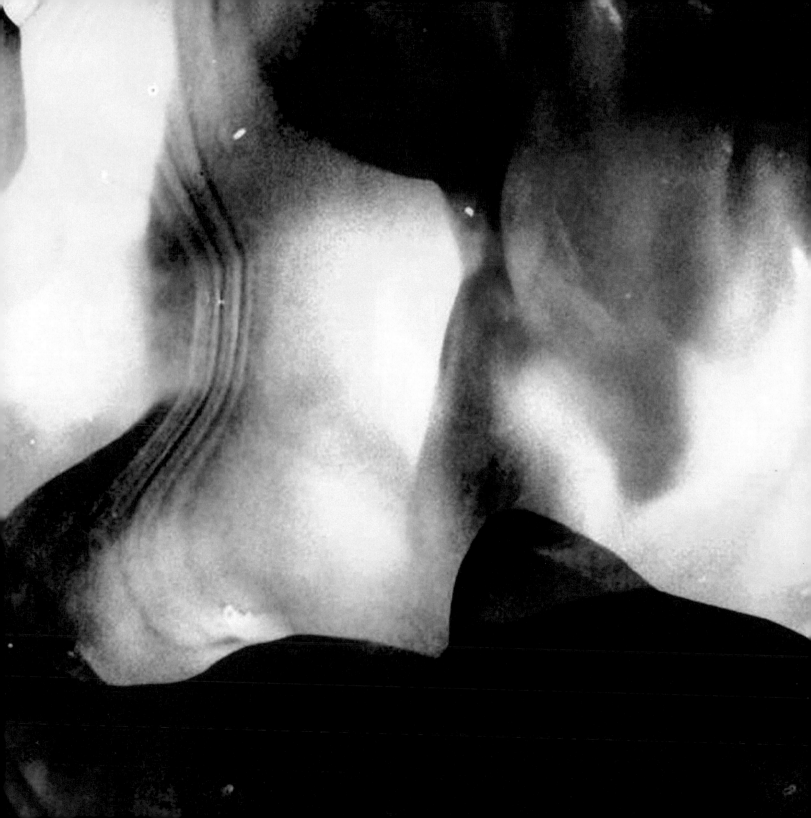

N is for navy

a navy trail

o is for Orange

an orange flame

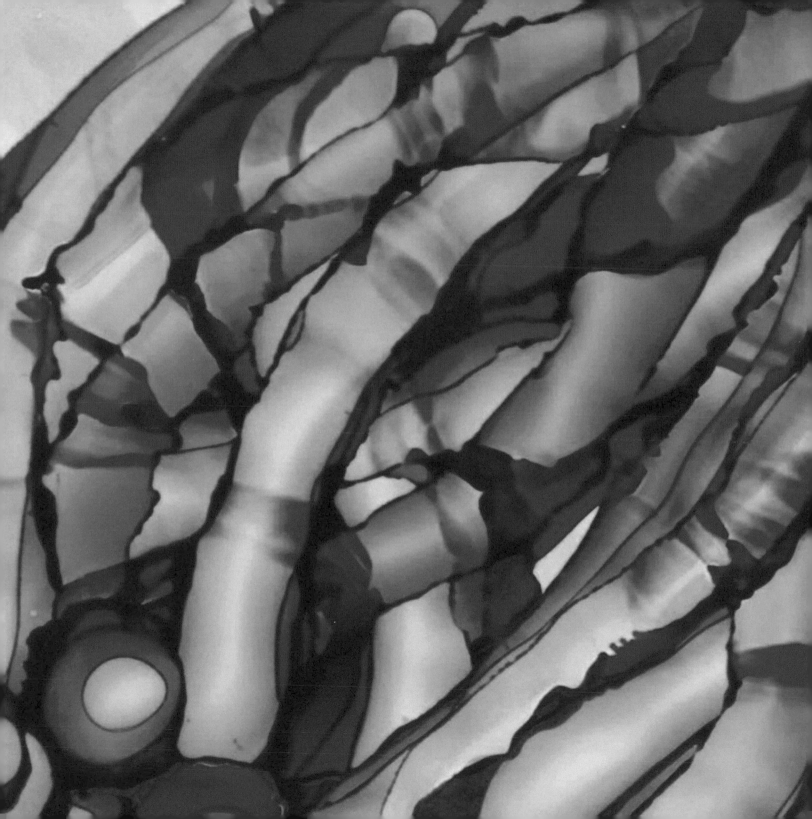

P is for purple

a purple rose

Q is for quartz

a quartz companion

R is for red

a red bed for gold

s is for silver

a silver night

T is for tangerine

a tangerine sun

u is for umber

an umber twist

v is for vermilion

a vermilion climb

w is for white

a white bubble wave

x is for xanthic

a xanthic mix

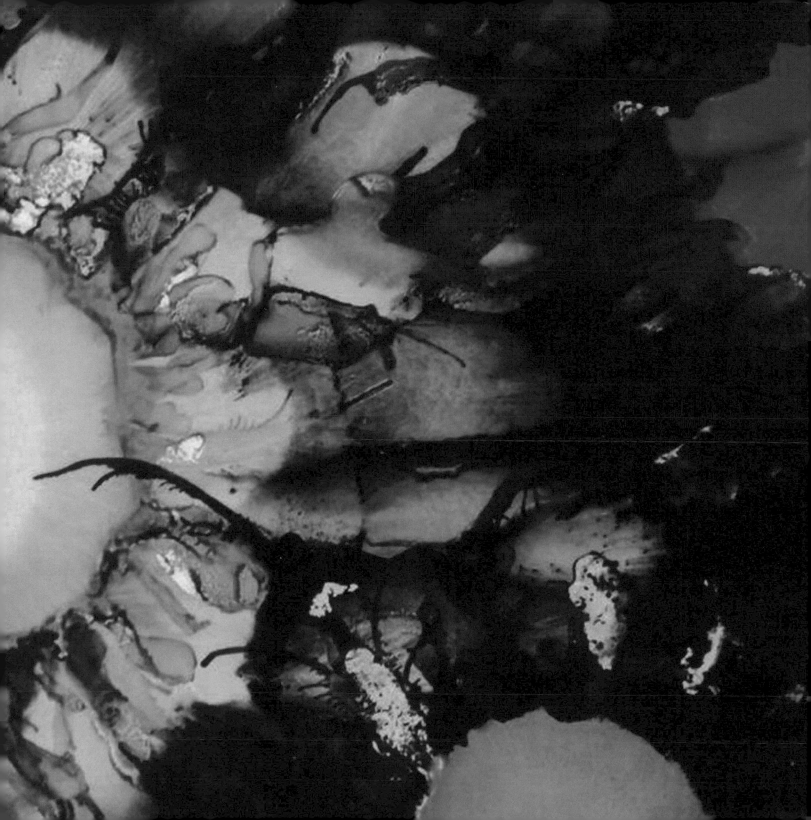

is for ellow

a ellow hello

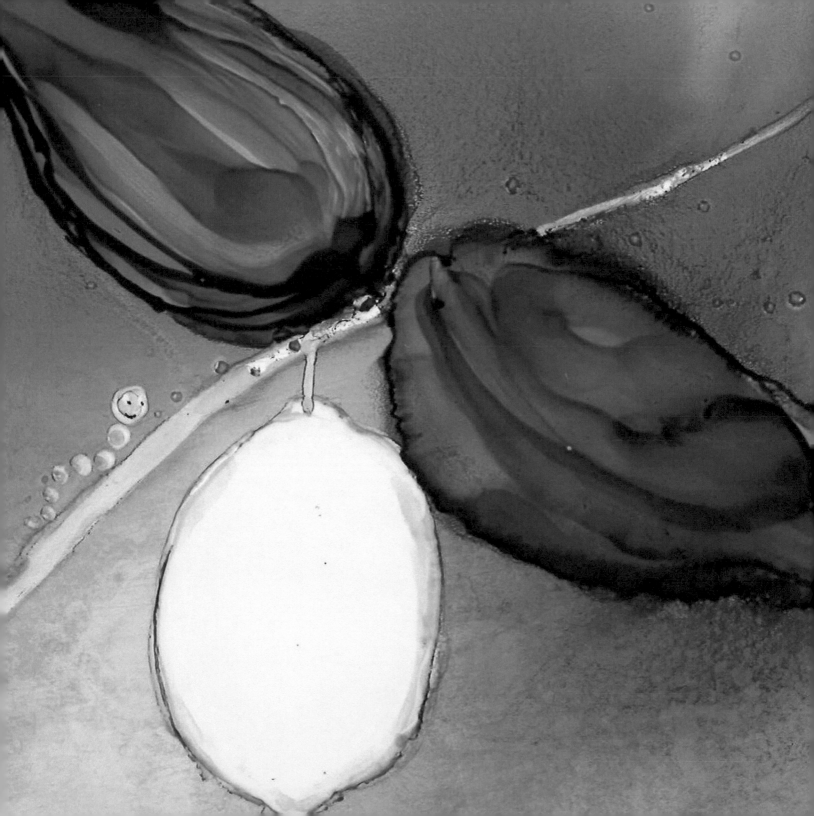

z is for zaffre

a zaffre goodbye

Color Names	Color Key	Pronunciation Guide	Rhymes
Azure	♥	/ăzh´ər/	(slant rhymes with *pleasure*)
Brass	♥	/brăs/	(rhymes with *glass*)
Cranberry	♥	/krăn´bĕr´ē/	(rhymes with *cherry*)
Denim	♥	/dĕn´ĭm/	(rhymes with *venom*)
Emerald	♥	/ĕm´rəld/	(slant rhymes with *trembled*)
Fuchsia	♥	/fyo͞o´shə/	(rhymes with *minutia*)
Green	♥	/grēn/	(rhymes with *screen*)
Heliotrope	♥	/hēl´yə´trōp´/	(rhymes with *antelope*)
Iceberg	♥	/īs´bûrg´/	(rhymes with *Gutenberg*)
Jasmine	♥	/jăz´mĭn/	(slant rhymes with *jazzmen*)
Kiwi	♥	/kē´wē/	(rhymes with *pee wee*)
Lilac	♥	/lī´lŏk´/	(rhymes with *block*)
Midnight	♥	/mĭd´nīt´/	(rhymes with *delight*)
Orange	♥	/ôr´ĭnj/	(slant rhymes with *storage*)
Purple	♥	/pûr´pəl/	(slant rhymes with *circle*)
Quartz	♥	/kwôrts/	(rhymes with *shorts*)
Red	♥	/rĕd/	(rhymes with *bed*)
Silver	♥	/sĭl´vər/	(slant rhymes with *pilfer*)
Tangerine	♥	/tăn´jər-ēn´/	(rhymes with *queen*)
Umber	♥	/ŭm´bər/	(rhymes with *slumber*)
Vermilion	♥	/vər-mĭl´yən/	(rhymes with *million*)
White	♡	/wīt/	(rhymes with *night*)
Xanthic	♥	/zăn´thĭk/	(slant rhymes with *romantic*)
Yellow		/yĕl´ō/	(rhymes with *marshmallow*)
Zaffre	♥	/zăf´ər/	(rhymes with *laugher*)

Note: A *slant rhyme* is an almost-rhyme.

Want to Make a Predictable Sentence Chart?

You can help children learn to read and write important high-frequency words by creating "predictable sentence" charts that are personalized for them and their friends. Just write the predictable sentences, one to a line, on a large poster board and put on the wall, for easy spelling reference, warm feelings, and smiles.

An *A Is for Azure* predictable sentence chart that teaches *I*, *like*, and color names could read as follows:

> Mrs. Leonard's Class " I Like Colors" Chart
>
> I like azure. (plus child's name & azure illustration card)
> I like brass. (plus child's name & brass illustration card)
> I like cranberry. (plus child's name & cranberry illustration card)
> I like denim. (plus child's name & denim illustration card)
> I like emerald. (plus child's name & emerald illustration card)
>
> ...and so on, for the whole class!

Stop in to **tweetspeakpoetry.com/literacyextras** for miniature reproductions of the illustrations in *A Is for Azure*, to print out and put on your predictable sentences chart.

About the Author

L.L. (Laura) Barkat is a books, parenting, and education contributor to *The Huffington Post* blog and the author of six books for grown-ups, including the popular title *Rumors of Water: Thoughts on Creativity & Writing*, which reveals the secrets of her writing journey—a journey she has joyfully shared with her daughters during their years of being educated at home and beyond. Her first memories of learning to read involve a grandma who taught her with colorful alphabet flash cards, two funny little British books about an ant and a bee, and a mother who read poetry to her daily. She loves color and has painted her dining room sunset yellow, because it makes her happy.

About the Illustrator

Donna Z. Falcone is an early childhood educator who, having once served in preschools and kindergartens, now dedicates her time to being an artist. Thanks in part to the influence of her artistic mom (Pat), Donna is passionate about helping teachers cultivate their inner artists and playful selves, as a way to bring energy and hope to their own lives and the lives of the children who they're privileged to nurture and inspire. Donna wishes to go to Italy someday, to the town of colors that first spoke its brilliant hope into her heart. Those colors now splash across tiles through inks that often go where they will, even as they play within certain bounds, much like children everywhere.

About the Publisher

T. S. Poetry Press is the sponsor of **tweetspeakpoetry.com**, where color and fun abounds— around the topics of poetry, writing, and lifelong literacy growth. The Press promotes "poetry for life" and "literacy for life" through free teaching and learning resources, books for grown-ups, and books for children. The publisher is committed to cultivating literacy as one way to create stronger connections across the generations—with co-learning materials that bring together grandparents and grandchildren, parents and children, and teachers and their students.

CPSIA information can be obtained at www.ICGtesting.com
Printed in the USA
LVIW01n1531130917
548610LV00009B/89

* 9 7 8 1 9 4 3 1 2 0 1 9 2 *